My Lover Feeds Me Grapefruit

Also by Mohja Kahf

Poetry
E-mails from Scheherazad
Hagar Poems

Fiction
The Girl in the Tangerine Scarf

Nonfiction
Western Representations of the Muslim Woman:
From Termagant to Odalisque

My Lover
Feeds Me Grapefruit

POEMS

Mohja Kahf

Press 53
Winston-Salem

Press 53, LLC
PO Box 30314
Winston-Salem, NC 27130

First Edition

A Tom Lombardo Poetry Selection

My Lover Feeds Me Grapefruit by Mohja Kahf
Winner of the 2020 Press 53 Award for Poetry

Library of Congress Control Number
2020930962

ISBN 978-1-950413-19-5

Acknowledgments

The author thanks the ediors of the publications where these poems first appeared.

Atlanta Review, Fall/Winter 2001, "Ramadan, My Beloved"

Banipal: Magazine of Modern Arab Literature, Issue 12, Autumn 2001, "My Lover Feeds Me Grapefruit"

Critical Muslim, Issue 21, 2016 "Ramadan S&M"; Issue 21, 2017, "Here It Is"

DontTalkToMeAboutLove: an Online Magazine Exploring Love In Fiction, Non-Fiction, Poetry And Art, 14 Sept., 2017, "Cigarette"

Literature and Belief, Volume 20.1, 2001, Center for the Study of Christian Values in Literature, Brigham Young University, "Garments"

Love, Inshallah: Fresh Perspectives on Love, 8 July 2013, "The Pleasure That It Is"; 6 Jan. 2014, "Manifesto for an Old-Fashioned Wanton"

Mizna: Prose, Poetry, and Art Exploring Arab America, Volume 4, Issue 2, Winter/Spring 2002, "Leaf"; Volume 6, Issue 1, 2004, "Kilimanjaran," "Hazelnut Harvest"

Paintbrush: a Journal of Contemporary Multicultural Literature, Issue 27, Spring 2000, "A Man's Chest"

Post Gibran: Anthology of New Arab American Writing, Khaled Mattawa and Munir Akash, ed., Syracuse University Press, 2000, "More Than One Way to Break a Fast"

Sukoon Magazine, July 2018, "Midnight Snack," "A Man Who Washes My Dishes"

Sustenance and Desire: A Food Lover's Anthology of Sensuality and Humor, Bascove, ed., David R. Godine Press, 2004, "Pears in the Time of Burnished Gold"

Thirteen Myna Birds, 27 July 2017, "Woman-Crisp"

Contents

Foreword by Rahat Kurd   xi

When I Come to You	3
My Lover Feeds Me Grapefruit	4
Alligators	5
The Pleasure That It Is	6
Never Mind	7
Manifesto for an Old-Fashioned Wanton	8
Eat, Eat	9
A Man Who Washes My Dishes	10
Jongleur	11
More Than One Way to Break a Fast	12
Concerns at a Conference	13
Kiss Me, You Fool	14
Pennies	15
Invocation	16
Hazelnut Harvest	17
One-Grape Days	18
Ramadan, My Beloved	19
Boardwalk	20
Wet Chastity	21
Baa	23
Woman-Crisp	24
Cigarette	26
Toe Ring Falls in Sleeve	28
Ramadan S&M	29
Censor	30
Death, My Best Friend Forever	31
River	32
Canoe	33
Lowering of the Gaze	36
Yard Work	37

A Man's Chest   38
Worship عبادة   39
Ramadan Granny Panties   41
Another One of the World's Liars   42
The Celtic God at the Waterfront Poetry Festival   43
Funnel Cake   44
The Rocks of Khor Fakkan   46
Hidden Date   49
Leaf   50
Missing You in the Music   51
Moonbopped   52
When You Come to Me   54
Kilimanjaran   55
Here It Is   56
A Man Like Green Onions   57
Wall   58
Olive Oil & Thyme زيت و زعتر   59
More about the Celtic God at the Waterfront Festival 60
Amnesty   61
Ramadan Godsend   62
When Love Feels Like Fingernails Cut Too Short   63
Pears in the Time of Burnished Gold   65
Winter Heat   66
To Eid   68
Bury Me in Arabic   69

Author's Note: Decolonial Broomsticks   73

Author Biography   77

Foreword by Rahat Kurd

In this radiant collection of love poems, Mohja Kahf makes a feast and a celebration, in language and of language. Everyone is invited: "Never drink while another is thirsty. You first. No, you. We could dance like this forever." From dizzying bursts of eros to wry acceptance of mortality, Kahf translates her robust Arabic literary lineage into the regal command: "Always multiply the gift." Pleasure shimmers off these pages with spiritual undertones, glancing subtly at Quran, at hadith. The opening poem, "When I Come to You," echoes a Hadith Qudsi in which God says, "When my worshipper comes to Me walking, I go to her running." With its joyful succession of images calling for reciprocity, this poem, and the collection, honor the mutual desire for union between Creator and creature as a foundation for expressions of human desire. From that generous place, we leap into lyric delight in the physicality of the erotic. It is the reader's task and reward to embrace "this beautiful clumsiness."

My Lover Feeds Me Grapefruit

When I Come to You

When I come to you running
come to me sprinting
When I come to you smiling
come to me laughing
When I come to you dancing
come to me clapping and stamping
When I come to you clowning
cartwheel across the boardwalk to me
Do you know how long it's taking
to learn this beautiful clumsiness?
When I come to you
rush to me, fly

My Lover Feeds Me Grapefruit

First he peels the grapefruit
The undulating rind descending fragrant
makes a hanging garden of Ninevah
Next he scrapes off the white
queensbread
making a little mound
of torn lace   the knife
wheedling
the little altar growing
till the grapefruit is bald
Then he pulls back the tender membrane
exposing rose-glistening
grapefruit flesh
wet wedges opening
between his fingers
the plate of my thighs shifting slightly
my tongue-tip snatching
pips from his palm
every little morsel containing
the slippery seed holy

Alligators

I wrestle with the alligator of your one thigh
and when I have subdued it
I wrestle with the alligator of the other
When the thrashing is over
the river is swollen and I
am mighty
satisfied

The Pleasure That It Is

In Ramadan, we spoon
innocent as children
We sleep with the door wide open

cocooned in Ramadan-time
its slow-ticking day, its blink-quick night
In Ramadan, we know that this

(your hand under my breast, the splay
of legs, the parted lips)
is not a prelude to anything
It is the pleasure that it is—
another one of Ramadan's
shy unbounded gifts

Never Mind

Remember when I said
I wanted to love you chastely?
I may have spoken hastily
Remember when I claimed
that pure love from afar
was all I was after?
I was daft, and you
if you believed me
dafter

Manifesto for an Old-Fashioned Wanton

I will be your wild mare
at night, but in the day
blush if you glimpse a nipple
through my blouse & look away

There's no feral depravity
you'd not drive me to in bed
Come morning, I'll hide in your chest
like a child from all I did

Eat, Eat

Eat as much as you love us.
  —Arab women's saying

See the oval platters over-sprinkled
with pistachio and glistening pine-nuts?
See the beds of saffron rice heaped
with dark and white meats embracing?
The squash and burghul soften,
home with garlic and cilantro

The gift, it teaches me generosity
Now I can give beyond measure

Never drink while another is thirsty—
You first. No, you. We could dance
like this forever

The eggplants
in a thousand ways
give their souls for us

Let the burst of pomegranate seeds
purple your mouth. Parsley is
so much more than a garnish
Eat, be satisfied and satisfy—
Tomorrow, I will be your guest

A Man Who Washes My Dishes

I love a man who clears my table
I love a man who knows how to use
a steel scouring brush on my pots
He brings out my shine

I love a man who washes my dishes
making soapy circles with his manly hands
around the curves of my delicate glassware
sliding lathery down the slimmest stem

I love a man who moves patiently
around my kitchen, turning like a deft spatula
remembering the places and purposes
of every latch, knob, and cubby

I love a man who stands up
in the tired aftermath of a meal
wiping the last counter, chasing
the last honeyed crumb into moist corners

I love a man not afraid to explore
the disposal blades with naked fingers
for the coiled peel of the final tangerine—
I love a man who washes my dishes

Jongleur

This is the dulcimer of my waist
you would be strumming if you were here

This is the curved lute of my neck
you would be plucking if you were near

This is the kamanja of my body
where the bow of your lips goes balladeer

the hawthorn blooms of my nights and thighs
when days grow long with you afar

More Than One Way to Break a Fast

After Hafsa bint al-Hajj

Your lips are dark, my love
and fleshy like a date
Sunset honeyslow
Black licorice, to wait

I have fasted, darling,
daythrough all Ramadan—
that tamarind, your mouth—
so near—the hours long

Grant one hibiscus kiss—
you know what milk reward
feeders of fasters gain
from our plummy Lord

The raisins soaked grow fat
The carob juice is poured
Kiss me—it's time, it's time!
And let us smorgasbord

Concerns at a Conference

My pressing concern is the raw intelligence
of tawny skin through the down on his arm
a total stranger seated inches ahead of me

during the keynote address. I am, moreover
very concerned about the lobe of his ear
a noose on which I'd like to hang myself

My urgent concern at the present time
is to stop myself taking a very small bite of—
so under my nose I can smell it—the furry peach of his neck

Kiss Me, You Fool

Yes, you
This is the poem
grabbing you by the collar
casting aside bikini talk
This is a poem, wet
with the fine spray of creativity
How can you look at me
lying here in the nude
glory of language
and just go on doing
what you do?
Take me—I want you to
read me again
and again, you fool

Pennies

I collect the coin
of your bitter-tasting copper
nipples
your body
flung
on my mat

Invocation

Come to me in the morning
when the face of the earth is still wet
Come to me in the evening
when the fumes subside into sweat
Stream down my body
Green and vine on my waist

Come like the ghost of dew
makes love to the pale maidengrass
Bounce over my gate like a red rubber ball
Land like a wet frog on my thighs
Come to me like the snowfall
makes the land virgin again

Come to me like a cat softly
Slip through my legs in the night
between my neck and my fright
Loop like a ring in my earlobe
with or without your disguise

Hazelnut Harvest

Here is your boyhood
running out to meet me
my girlhood skipping
to greet you in the orchard

Do you feel the meadow
when you move through me?
I feel the season ripening

I taste hazel trees
in your arms and days
of hazelnut shelling
What do you taste in me?

This harvest pours
through my body—
take, glean
this gift, grace
heaping, husking
hulls splitting
yielding, my hair curling
over your brown ground

One-Grape Days

When I met you
—the passion, the possibility—
I couldn't eat—a single grape
snatched off the table in passing
was enough to go on for the day
I was feasting inwardly

Ramadan, My Beloved

I came to you in the hungriest hour
water cupped in my hand
stealthy as Zamzam to Hajar
angelfood to Maryam
dateflesh at sunset
nudged between parched lips
You put your lips to the rim of my hand
Remember me in Ramadan
when you eat and drink

Boardwalk

I skip between your kisses
like a kid on the boardwalk
Put your arm around my waist
Be my plush purple ring toss win

I clutch tickets, your sticky words
Here come the unicyclists
spinning blue and gold
Here I am in a silver sequin bikini

backflipping at a kajillion feet
both hands outstretched
for meeting your hands
no net

Wet Chastity

After Wallada bint al-Mustakfi

So many men I'd love to have fucked
if I wasn't so committed to mono-amorousness
In the name of the Compassionate, the Merciful
if I make it to heaven off all this fucking chastity
I want those men there by the rivers of milk and honey
Remember, God, that brawny brown Egyptian
standing with massive legs, pillars upholding
the grand staircase of the grand mosque of my teen years?
The sadfaced Sefardic guitarist in the Hell's Kitchen café
would that he'd played me with his nimble fingers
And the Ghanaian golden prince in the suburbs, his arms full
of groceries, under whose feet rivers of orange juice flowed
Don't act like you don't know who I mean, God
just because I cast my eyes away after my one freebie look
Allahumma grant me that ice-blond repairman, my first married year
like a Viking in his great dirt-caked workboots
Bestow upon me the tall Pakistani techie
his sexy dark eyes under one connected eyebrow
his geek sleeves rolled up over arms equally sexy and dark
Plus the pale white professor with the epic lips
who red-lined my fresh college fantasies
I'd like to reserve a seminar table in heaven for him
And those three long-lashed Saudi men in the Mecca mall, so shallow
I wouldn't want to have two back-to-back conversations with them—
I'd say, "Just shut up and roll around in the heavenly bed with me
you long-lashed khaleeji men whose lustrous black eyes
shine juxtaposed to pristinely white headdresses"

O Lord of the Kaba, who feedeth against hunger and preserveth my body
against corruption, please save a banquet of men for me
'n tell whichever angels are in charge of the sex

to be recording them all in your big black book in paradise
all the forbidden fruits of my earthly forbearance
forgetting none, and multiplying my reward merrily
like row upon row of silky corn on the cob
verily, verily, verily, verily

Baa

I'm a lost sheep
grazing on the plains
of your hairy chest
muscled knolls
low belly lands
Pull me in with your crook

Woman-Crisp

Can we speak together over time and space
naked of our names?

This is crazy
I'm growing fins to swim out and meet you

Say yes: this is transformation
My skin slipping away
Yesterday, I misplaced my Self

Say you have been entrusted with a packet
a word to give to me
I am ready

Text me from your Galaxy
Message me from your apartment of fire
inside the sun

Hurry! answer me
I need a voice to jump toward
so I won't break in two
from the middle of my spinal cord
to dangle in the sky, a broken crescent

I'm shaking off the lie
Blue sparks fly from my hair
My fingernails curl off

I sizzle in the round black
frying pan of cosmic void
Hurry! before I fry
into burnt woman-crisp

All that needs to be written
is a single word

Cigarette

I want to be your cigarette
so your fingertips will touch me

I want to be your cigarette
so your lips will ply my length
now clenched, now sneering

I want to be your cigarette
so your flame will graze and light
my crushed leaves, tightly packed

I want to be your cigarette
your hands cupped around me
your teeth bared, your nostrils
when they scent me flaring

I want to be your cigarette
so you will suck my smoke
and your hair and chest and shirt
will smell of me

I want to be your cigarette
so you will be unable
despite heroic efforts
ever to quit me

I want to be your cigarette
so you will roll my last gasps
between your skilled hands
then snuff me among the ashes

And when you press, fumbling
your breast pocket again
desperate I want to be
your next cigarette

Toe Ring Falls in Sleeve

After al-Dahna' bint Masshal

Five months I haven't struggled with your chestbarrel
unlocked the spigots of your wrists, smelled your tobacco nape
Come straight from the airplane to our bed and make it judder
Don't stop till my toe ring plops into my sleeve

Ramadan S&M

Coffeeless and sleep-deprived, I stagger
into the first day with my face
tripping over my shoes
Ramadan, why you do me this way?
On the second day, I'm haggard
horny and bad-breathed
needing a drag, and a drink
a boot leather taste in my mouth
Ramadan, what I ever do to you?
The body whines its need
If I can't have bread and sex and chocolate
let me at least have sleep
Even against that refuge
Ramadan raises its whip
Hour after hour on the rack of Ramadan
day after captive day
the appetite is dulled
down to a whimper
until

my will
tempered on your stone
upswings sharper edged—
Ramadan, you sado-masochistic
driver, don't make me love you
in the final stretch, in my triumph
of Self mastery

Censor

You are not a muse
You are on the side of the Inquisition
Okay, maybe Inquisitor is too grand
You crush like a bureaucrat
with a nondescript motion
when no one is looking
convincing yourself
that you squelch for the common good

Death, My Best Friend Forever

Death pinkie-promised always to be my best friend
Yes, Death and I enjoy long walks on the beach
Here's photo-booth pictures of us
laughing and making faces
People badmouth Death, but she's really
not stand-off-ish or scary once you get to know her
not drama queen like Illness
or clique-ish like Suffering and Loneliness
in their black turtlenecks
Death is a down-to-earth chick
Why, she could be in a sturdy blue flannel shirt
a surprise guest at Thanksgiving, a random bullet
Arm in arm, Death and I walk to the bus stop
she whispering in my ear, "Everything concrete is really so fragile"
I take my kid to karate, drop off a toaster oven
at the mail station; the flood of mundaneness never ends
but with Death at my side, none of it is boring
She gives a shine to my everything
Death reminds me to ready my shroud
like the Blessed Fatima, who used to practice
lying in her grave-sheet nightly
"Best friend I ever had," Death says of Fatima
with me standing right there! It's okay
sometimes I too forget about Death's presence
even as she hovers polishing
my mirrors, wanting me to see
clearly, blemish and beauty
Aside from obsessive-compulsive mirror polishing, Death
is a messy housekeeper. "Lower your threshold for grime"
Death always says to me. "There's not enough time
for all that cleaning. Kiss your daughter's cheek
before I turn you and her over to the worms"
What a friend, what a sadistic bitch

River

Where is the man who doesn't need
to be giant or god
but becomes river
rushing down into the canyon of her
frothing greedily
wetting and whetting the henna-red rock

Canoe

Your chest is the bark
of a canoe
in my capsized night
I find your nipples
knots in the wood
and you draw me in
dripping
to the dry hollow

Siesta

Two pigeons flutter, settle
on sun-weathered slats:
my breasts nesting in your chest

Garments

*for they [spouses] are garments unto you
and you are garments unto them*
—Quran 2:187

What kind of garment will you be?
Maybe I slip the silk of you across my belly
It has taken me these centuries
to name my desire apart from your desire for me

Gabardine, structure for a breast to lean against?
Workday wool, checked madras
sensible muslin gathering my waist—
what kind of garment unto me

the back of your neck pharoanal linen
Complex cashmere, sarcenet
glint thread of ego striping damask, we
ribbon and chemise. If you are my garment
what kind of garment will you be?

Lowering of the Gaze

Tell the believing men to lower of their gazes and guard their
orifices . . . . and tell the believing women to lower of their
gazes and guard their orifices
                              —Quran 24:30 & 31

I love the man of lowered gaze
and the woman of lowered gaze
And I love the man who looks hungrily
and the woman who looks hungrily
I have been the man with the hungry gaze
and the man of iron restraint
whose eyes leave what is covered, covered
I have been the woman with the ravenous mouth
and the woman with the disciplined will
like an axe sharply splitting wood
like an axe at the moment it is lifted
poised, in that pause before descent
And I am the gaze and the pause
and the wood that is split

Yard Work

This bed of leaves
begs to be crackled

Quick, the trees
are looking the other way—

Pull out your rake
Make mulch of me

A Man's Chest

How come no one ever writes about a man's chest
that forested mountain and its bluffs and crags
where a lover can hide
from the city and every fanged creature?

How come no one ever writes about a man's belly
that smooth river and how limpid
waters run low, where a lover
can wade barefoot?

How come no one ever writes about a man's waist
that belt loop for a woman's fingers
that catches her in its buckle?

How come no one ever writes about a man's hips
how the arms of a lover
girdle them like a seamstress hemming
a gorgeous dress?

How come no one ever writes about a man's thighs
those rugged cliffs and how we shudder
every muscle to climb
their rocky sides, foothold after foothold
up to the dizzying heights
between his

collarbones, those magnificent promontories
where finally the earth opens up its mist
and there is a fine place
far from the city below
and every fanged creature
no one writes about
in a man's chest

Worship عبادة

Kissing is ablution
grazing three times each: nape
inner elbow, ear conch

The hands rise and drop
shoulders to hips
signal intention

Thighs open the prayer
the night worth a thousand months
final finger movements subtle, knuckled

Crowning, the cry
testifies
to truth and its messenger

Belly slack on belly
peace, peace
until the mounting of the dawn

The Long Way Home

A man's body at night is a highway shimmering
in the headbeams of heavy trucks
your hand firm on the steering wheel
precise, making the turn around his earlobe
the hills rippling like muscle
a sharp veer into uncontrolled intersections
a rumble in the earthbeat
You drive the long way home

Ramadan Granny Panties

Sure, it says in the Quran
that there's no harm
to go unto your spouse
when the fasting's done
but by then the body's wilted
the sap is gone
God, that Sly One
knows what She's doing
beaching the beast into its calm
You're lucky to get lucky
once or twice all month long
So get the big white cotton
granny panties from the bottom
of the drawer, girls—Ramadan
is not a time for thongs

Another One of the World's Liars

I am just another one of the world's liars
believe me
I have a few charms
worn-out peddler's trinkets
with grand names like beauty
friendship, truth, passion
—and this one's a real item, sometimes
I even buy it myself: love
Check my record; odds
are not in your favor
that I won't sell out
my goods, bolt by night
deny you three times
before the cock has crowed
Consider this fair warning:
never fall for my spiel
If you do
and end up with a huge bill
for damage done
never forgive me

The Celtic God at the Waterfront Poetry Festival

Each forearm was a muscular sonnet
Each pectoral iambically stressed
His hands drawled like the working classes
Knuckles like steel mills and ballads
His thighs were great founding epics
His chest a pagan Norse saga
packed stubborn with angst and boast
His belly was villanelle
and when he swiveled from the waist
with the sweep of an arm Mississippi
his tee-shirt hiked up a rondel
Each of his nipples under it
was the nest of a tiny bird haiku
His Whitman shoulders
whittled down to a Sandburg waist
I just know that bulge was a canto
thick with itself like Pound
hirsute with obscure allusions
His behind when he turned—
like when you close a book, satisfied
His face was all anguish and Hart Crane
and hard drink and hard love and hard luck
His jaw was set Irish and Yeats
His eyes winked e.e. cummings
I stopped by lovely woods to look

Funnel Cake

You feed me lies like funnel cakes
and I in the starchy frock
Mother warned me to keep clean
I throw up high on the ferris wheel
of your daredevil joy, bad boy
I come home with one shoe
my camisole smudged
from your greasy paperbag grins
and I was a girl at her window
alone and far from the feast

Naked Toast

When I am toast and butter
eat me like toast and butter
Don't wish I was cream and honey
Don't scrape off my burnt edges
Imagine what you could do
with a woman in your arms
naked as toast

The Rocks of Khor Fakkan

I need to peel the earth like an apple
until my fullness dilates
my breast-tips run with milk

until the crescent moon cracks
snaps her spine in two
and falls on my verranda

I need a hard booze, I need a masked lover
I need a different man in every port
I need a new religion

like redhot coals on my chest
something with bells so clangorous
my head will hurt for days

I need to speak a foreign tongue
that tastes like mulberry man-nipple
to make me forget my ugly lexicon

I need lethal hair like Medusa
clothes in poisonous colors
I need to learn flamenco

and love men who are bad for me
And after I become this new woman
I need to abandon her in Rio

and become a virgin again
or a dominatrix, I haven't decided
I need a carnival lovemaking

something that will exhaust me
so thoroughly I won't have to think
I need a new noose, something

that knows the shape of my neck
a guitar to serenade me
something so beautiful-sad

it will keep me at the balcony
until my period flows like the moon
rilling into the river

and I am either baptized to new life
in the icy froth of Cape Chelyuskin
or dashed to death against the steaming rocks of Khor Fakkan

Autumn Breathing Hard

Wind blows in the ear
of the thick-waisted tree
It blushes bright red
and shimmies off its panties
Giant invisible lovers
lift shifting leaves
like crisp bedsheets
Autumn is naked and chill
Warm with the breath of desire
we huddle soft as goslings
placid as mice in a nest

Hidden Date

The oblong brown
cavern moist and sweet
where date flesh parts
into two maybe four
delicious complexities
where the pit meets
the tongue before you eat
when the sun goes down

Leaf

I don't understand clock hands anymore
Weekdays—what were their names?
I've shot back into primal time
before Tammuz and Thor

I comprehend Red. I speak Leaf
I know why Gilgamesh cried
I fathom sex—
for the first time, really—
how it is not a technical matter at all
but a fractal of infinity

I am living in indigo
See it smeared on my cheekbone?
How do I keep functioning
in the world of clocks and names?
Colleagues head down the hall to talk to me
as if they didn't see the winged Zanë
breaking into flight around us
How can I answer?
I only speak Leaf

Missing You in the Music

I am missing you in the music
and I am missing you in the morning cigarette
and I am missing you in the coffee and the cream
Yes it is morning here already
time to be missing you
And I am missing you in the afternoon
in the baskets of farmers' market blueberries
It is June, it is berry time
it is a very missing-you time
And I am missing you in my evening tea
It is missing you o'clock
and I am missing you in the gurgle of water
spouting from the spout of the missing you

Moonbopped

The moon bopped me this morning
All I know is I step outside and there it sprawls
        loafing
in the neon pink sky where it shouldn't be
and suddenly I somersault into the ionosphere
green antennae shoot from my ears
picking up radio signals from Venus
        scratchy Roma violins
        and Godzilla footage from Japan
Today
for the first time
ever
in the world
there is lightning crackling through me
Can you hear, can you hear me sizzle?
Stop me before all the light bulbs pop
Stop me before my front porch daffodils
bloom and burst and droop
like time-lapse photography fasterfaster
        bloomburstdroop
        bloomburst like fireworks
I hold my head to keep it attached
haven't touched food for days
And I can't
stop
clicking
        these Moroccan castanets
        that have grown
        out of my fingers
        overnight

I eat clouds like lime-green Jersey taffy
I'm a Kahlo watermelon in vermillion
Watch me blurrrr into a million dragon-
        flies in green or cerullian
I'm the frog that zaps the dragonfly
        Zzt. Urp. I open my mouth
        and schools of fat fish swim out
        in rainbow ribbons, light
        from stained glass windows
I swing from the gothic spire of the world
like a spider from her flimsy thread, like Michaelangelo
when his workmen forget the dolly crank and he careens
twirling into chapel walls and smearing paint
        What kind of cosmic icecubedownmyback
        is this?
All my careful work is ruined
        all because the moon
lumped me a great big shiner just today
        bopped me clear
into the electron-humping subatomic Quark-o-sphere

When You Come to Me

You come to me
My stopped clocks tick again
Water unfreezes in the garden hose
Little red lights begin blinking on the DVD player
the one I haven't been able to program for years
Suddenly classic Technicolor movies blast
Lamps I don't remember buying
flicker symphonies and burn
my hands electric

Kilimanjaran

The proud giraffes of my breasts
will eat none but high leaf
of your chest

Here It Is

Here it is Ramadan
and I forgot to pray
I can think only of you

Here it is iftar
and I forgot to eat
banqueting on a joy
not at this table

Here it is nightfall
and I forgot the lightswitch
a whole chandelier
brilliant in my ribcage

Here it is dawn
and I've forgotten—
what is it again
that I'm to do sunrise?

Oh yes: slip away
die
come back to life—
Here it is

A Man Like Green Onions

You hurt the palate. You are not
now, and have never been, nice
Your children run from you,
do you notice? Like a knifed
onion, you make your wife cry
You browbeat most
the ones you love most. I make
complex plans to avoid you
Nonetheless at noisy meals
I miss the bite of salted onions
amid the spoons of mild rice

Wall

Your heart is a wall on which I knocked
looking for a door, a latch
a windowsill, a flowerpot

Everything I brought to the wall dried up
and blew away for lack of answer:
tulip bulbs, my worry for you, some children

Sometimes I pounded it with my fists
smashed my forehead on it
blamed myself for not having the passcode
hated myself
hated hating myself—started over
willed patience, got advice
cried in a heap against its brick
without getting a stir
so many night-after-nights

It's a wall.
There is no way in.

Now that I've made the choice to leave
your heart suddenly has a gate
You fling it open for the first time
but I'm gone

Olive Oil & Thyme   زيت و زعتر

We have dipped the breadscrap into the small bowl
of olive oil, making it moist and ready
Now we dip it into the companion dish
of sesame, ground thyme, sumac
the zest a little different each blend
familiar like our lifelong friendship
never the same flavor twice

More about the Celtic God at the Waterfront Festival

His deltoids,
I forgot to tell you
about his deltoids:
he may have been speaking
into the mic quite reasonably
but the animals
in the back of his bare upper arms
—I could see them from where I was sitting—
were fanged and open-jawed
and lunging straight at me

Amnesty

Visiting the foreign country of you
I was ambushed at your navel base
Detained by a kiss without warrant
Now I face extrajudicial elation
Geneva does not sanction
the unconventional weapon of your grin
Machiavellian, I accuse. However
I demand that you release me never

Ramadan Godsend

I love my period
In Ramadan, I love it more
Menses becomes the shore
I'm swimming for, my island reprieve
When the sea of fasting days
towers tidal waves
I scan the horizon—down there
for the thin red rope
my last-hour hope
before fasting fatigue
drags me into the undertow
Was that it? No. Is this it? Oh
come to me, thou full of grace
thou moon of face, my fons vitae
my lovely blood, be thou mine
salvation every twenty-eight days
or twenty-five or twenty-nine
give me thy hammock sway
become my white-aproned waiter
bearing tall cool drinks
appear and grant me holiday
Flow, baby, flow

When Love Feels Like Fingernails Cut Too Short

Don't tear me jaw from jaw and jump inside me
Don't mend me where I'm unraveling and sew
my seams together with your seams so tightly, Ow
Leave a piece of Self for me in the refrigerator
Don't eat me all, darling, chocolate as I may be

Midnight Snack

My man's armpits
are peanut butter—
the creamy kind
They make my mouth sticky
&
his pecs two toasted wheats

Pears in the Time of Burnished Gold

Take for your sickness from your health,
and for your poverty from your wealth
    —Prophet Muhammad,
        peace and blessings be upon him

You bring me pears
The juice runs down your fingers
How long has it taken me to realize
that this is the place
these are the times
which if one day there is a paradise
we will look back upon and say
Yes, we drank a little of this wine
We tasted, yes, of this before

You bring me pears
They are so ripe the knife curves
around the tender core
in a pear-cutting ballet
Your hands are whole
We have water and good health
I am suddenly aware
how everything around us is burnished gold

You bring me pears
You houri, if houris can be men
You lean toward me, hold me in your eyes
and I afraid to let go my breath
From my armchair, in the ordinary light
it seems as if your jeans are green brocade
embossed with silver as, moon among men
you orbit me

Winter Heat

Icy toes
continents apart over
frozen alpine zones
we laughing warm
each other's chittering bones

Domna

He phones me at seven a.m. on Sunday
wrapping his silken voice around my throat
"What are you, crazy?" I rasp in the receiver
"You know I am the Queen of Decadence
and never get up until day has made obeisance
Besides, I can't talk now. My other lover's here
his limbs dangling all over me"
Only my book in my bed
hardcover digging into my hipflesh
It's good to be cruel to a man sometimes,
makes him sharper. Especially when
he wakes me and his voice is way too sexy
I hang up on him, the phone cord twisted
around my bronzen upper arm
like the deadly snake bracelets
the great goddess Ishtar concocted
poison for her jeweled eye

To Eid

None of that Ramadan loftiness
seems to rub off on me, baby—
I talk a good show about victory
over the slopping trough of desire
and I can pull it off (maybe)
until the end of a fasting day
until the end of the month (if
you give me my menstrual vacation)
but as soon as the clock hand ticks
that sunset minute, honey, as soon
as that cannon booms
my inner pig charges out of its pen
rutting and grunting. No good
as a saint, I'm great as a sinner
God bless me! and you! and all
womankind and man, and our appetites—
Here's to Eid, I squeal, here's to Eid!

Bury Me in Arabic

"Morning of goodness to you"
—"Morning of goodnesses"
Or add flowers: "morning of roses"
Always multiply the gift—

"welcome" to "two welcomes"
"a hundred welcomes and kinship and ease"
Keep offering tray after tray of words

When someone fixes your engine
passes food, serves you in any way
say "May your hands be whole and healthy"
They echo "god keep you healthy and hale"

Wishing a sneezer "mercy" is a three-step dance
They reply "guidance and rightness of mind"
You match "guidance for you and me both"
When you cough you get "health"; top it off
"health and vigor!" or raise it "two healths!"

"Luxury" you tell someone fresh-skinned from bath
"Luxury back" the wet connecting your freckles
to their body's glow wordstreams you miss when they go

Served coffee? Say "always"
for "may you drink it always with joy"
—envision endless espresso streams at weddings
Just don't blurt "always" at condolences
when bitter coffee is served—
that wishes them always sorrow

There is one phrase
"May you bury my bones"
spoken only by kin in whose grave
you will, come a day, shovel dirt with whole hands—
it is supreme love
and has no utterable answer

Author's Note: Decolonial Broomsticks

Arab women have an abundance of poetic foremothers. The fat roster of hundreds of Arab women who write eros includes three women mentioned epigraphically in this book:

- Al-Dahna' bint Masshal, الدهناء بنت مسحل may have lived ca. early 700s CE in the Arabian peninsula. Reportedly she writes:

> Kissing squeezing sniffing won't
> win me over, she moans
> You've got to pound me out of my woes
> till my toe ring falls in my sleeve

- Wallada bint al-Mustakfi, ولادة بنت المستكفي 1001-1091 CE. Flamboyant scion of a defunct royal family in Cordoba, she mentored young women from impoverished families. Some became poets (including one named "Mohja," after whom I am named). Classical Arabic anthologies say Wallada composes these couplets embroidered on her sleeves:

> Beyond doubt, I am fit for magnificent heights
> So I jaunt my jaunts and I rove my roves
> I lavish the gift of my cheek on my beau
> And on craving lover my kiss bestow

- Hafsa bint al-Hajj, حفصة بنت الحاج 1135-1190 CE, made her livelihood teaching daughters of aristocratic families in Morocco. She writes, abuzz with more wordplay than I can translate:

> Those lips I laud; I know first-hand
> they're worth praise, I do not lie
> It's fair to say I sip from them
> buttery mouthfuls, finest wine

This richesse goes unnoticed in Western narratives which pity Arab women one minute for being too sexualized, the next for being sexually repressed. Sensuality is not more essential to Arab women than to other people, nor do Arab women need instruction in writing pleasure. Like Wallada, Hafsa, al-Dahna, and women before and after them in Arabic literature, we jaunt our jaunts. Arab women inherit no more patriarchy than women with European ancestry nor less. Nor less, but snarled by imperialist violence on Arab bodies. So no matter how feminist and liberal a white savior take on Arab women's poetry may be, such a reading aligns with racist imperialist heteropatriarchy. Instead of listening.

Writers of color are not all one thing nor are Arab women, but most of us know first-hand that the liberal gaze can recuperate our invisibility while looking right at our pages. How can we recover the sensual, along with the spiritual weft that is deeply woven into it, on our own terms? How can we sip buttery lips in a diaspora language that makes imperialist porn of our bodies? How can I, plus the roving writing crowd of Arab women alongside me, write the body within a world that wreaks violence on brown and black bodies? We sweep paths through paradoxes to make the magnificent spaces our creativity merits.

My sisters Wallada, Hafsa, and al-Dahna gamely help me to ply the decolonizing broom. Swish, swish (a job never finished). Cheeky, they lavish knowledge of lips. Toe rings ping. We break out sesame cookies for lively samar. Listen, you are invited.

Mohja Kahf   مهجة قحف